Pebble Plus
Presidential Biographies

Abraham Lincoln

by Erin Edison

Consulting Editor: Gail Saunders-Smith, PhD

Consultant:
Sheila Blackford
Librarian, Scripps Library
Managing Editor, *American President*
Miller Center, University of Virginia

CAPSTONE PRESS
a capstone imprint

Pebble Plus is published by Capstone Press,
1710 Roe Crest Drive, North Mankato, Minnesota 56003.
www.capstonepub.com

Library of Congress Cataloging-in-Publication Data
Edison, Erin.
Abraham Lincoln / by Erin Edison.
p. cm.—(Pebble plus. Presidential biographies)
Includes bibliographical references and index.
Summary: "Simple text and full-color photographs describe the life of Abraham Lincoln"—Provided by publisher.
ISBN 978-1-4296-8735-5 (library binding)
ISBN 978-1-62065-316-6 (ebook PDF)
1. Lincoln, Abraham, 1809–1865—Juvenile literature. 2. Presidents—United States—Biography—Juvenile literature. I. Title.
E457.905.E45 2013
973.7092—dc23
[B] 2011049857

Editorial Credits
Erika L. Shores, editor; Sarah Bennett, designer; Wanda Winch, media researcher; Kathy McColley, production specialist

Photo Credits
Alamy: North Wind Picture Archives, 5, 9; Corbis: Bettmann, 7, 13, 15, 19; Library of Congress: Prints and Photographs Division, cover, 1, 11, 17, 21

Note to Parents and Teachers

The Presidential Biographies series supports national history standards related to people and culture. This book describes and illustrates the life of Abraham Lincoln. The images support early readers in understanding the text. The repetition of words and phrases helps early readers learn new words. This book also introduces early readers to subject-specific vocabulary words, which are defined in the Glossary section. Early readers may need assistance to read some words and to use the Table of Contents, Glossary, Read More, Internet Sites, and Index sections of the book.

Printed in the United States of America in North Mankato, Minnesota.
122019 003058

Table of Contents

Early Years

Abraham Lincoln helped end slavery in the United States. The future president was born February 12, 1809, in Kentucky. At age 7, Abraham and his family moved to Indiana. There he chopped wood and plowed fields.

born in Kentucky

1809

Abraham could not go to school very often. His family needed him to help at home.

But Abraham wanted to learn.

He spent much of his free time reading.

born in Kentucky

1809

Life in Illinois

At age 21, Abraham moved to Illinois. He ran a store and worked on riverboats. He split wood to make fence rails. Abraham was very tall and thin, but he was strong. He also was fair and kind. People called him Honest Abe.

Abraham liked politics.
He was elected to the Illinois
House of Representatives in 1834.
He also studied to become a lawyer.
In 1842 he married Mary Todd.
They had four sons, but three
of them died young.

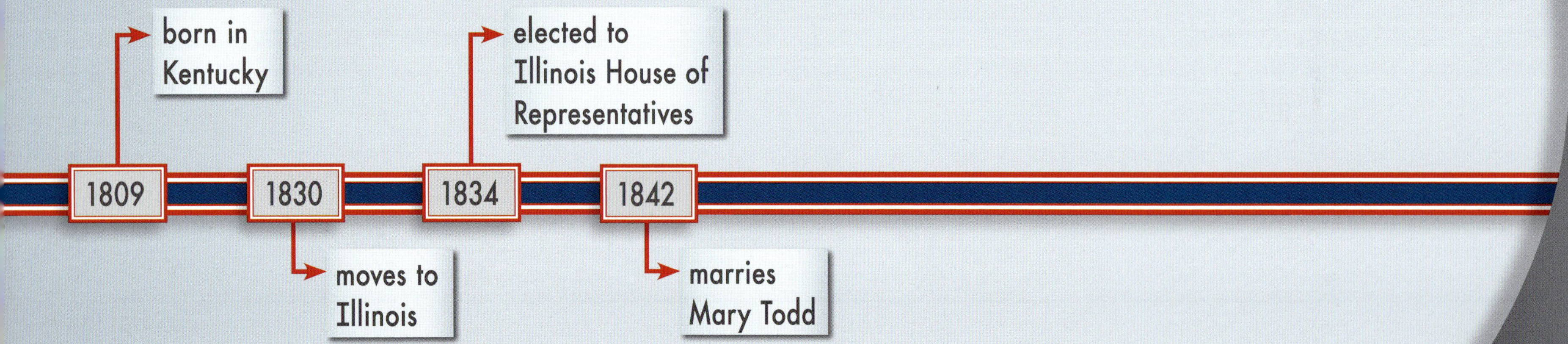

Mary and Abraham with their sons Robert and Thomas (Tad) around 1864

In 1846 Abraham was elected to represent Illinois in the U.S. Congress. Later, Abraham returned to Illinois and became one of the state's best lawyers. The issue of slavery caused Abraham to become interested in politics again.

- 1809 — born in Kentucky
- 1830 — moves to Illinois
- 1834 — elected to Illinois House of Representatives
- 1842 — marries Mary Todd
- 1846 — elected to U.S. Congress

Some southern states allowed slavery. Northern states did not. Senator Stephen Douglas wanted each state to decide if slavery was legal. Abraham said slavery was wrong. He wanted all Americans, not each state, to decide. The two men debated the issue.

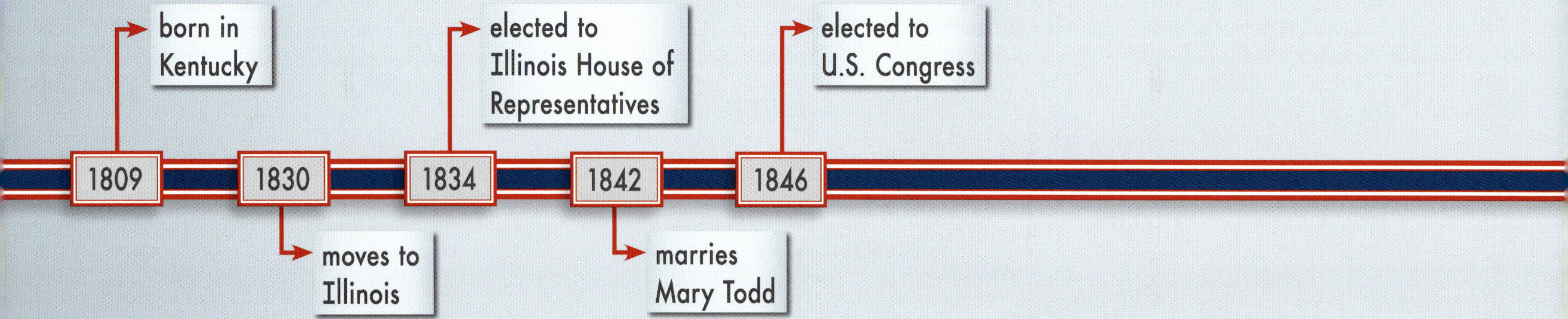

ILLINOIS BORN UNDER THE ORDINANCE OF '87
"WESTWARD THE STAR OF EMPIRE TAKES ITS WAY,
"THE GIRLS LINK ON TO LINCOLN,
THEIR MOTHERS WERE FOR CLAY."
ABE THE
THE LITTLE GIANT CHAWING UP OLD ABE
FREE TERRITORIES AND FREE MEN,
FREE PULPITS AND FREE PREACHERS.
FREE PRESS AND A FREE PEN,
FREE SCHOOLS AND FREE TEACHERS.

President Lincoln

Many people heard about the debates. They thought Abraham would make a good president. He was elected the 16th U.S. president in 1860. Soon southern states were fighting northern states in the Civil War (1861–1865).

- 1809 — born in Kentucky
- 1830 — moves to Illinois
- 1834 — elected to Illinois House of Representatives
- 1842 — marries Mary Todd
- 1846 — elected to U.S. Congress
- 1860 — elected 16th U.S. president

Abraham's inauguration on March 4, 1861

Abraham wrote and spoke boldly about keeping the country together and ending slavery. He signed the Emancipation Proclamation in 1863. This paper promised freedom to slaves. In April 1865 the North won the war.

- 1809 — born in Kentucky
- 1830 — moves to Illinois
- 1834 — elected to Illinois House of Representatives
- 1842 — marries Mary Todd
- 1846 — elected to U.S. Congress
- 1860 — elected 16th U.S. president
- 1863 — signs Emancipation Proclamation

Remembering Lincoln

A man named John Wilkes Booth was angry the South lost. He shot and killed Abraham. Many people believe Abraham was the greatest president. He kept the United States together as one country. He brought about the end of slavery.

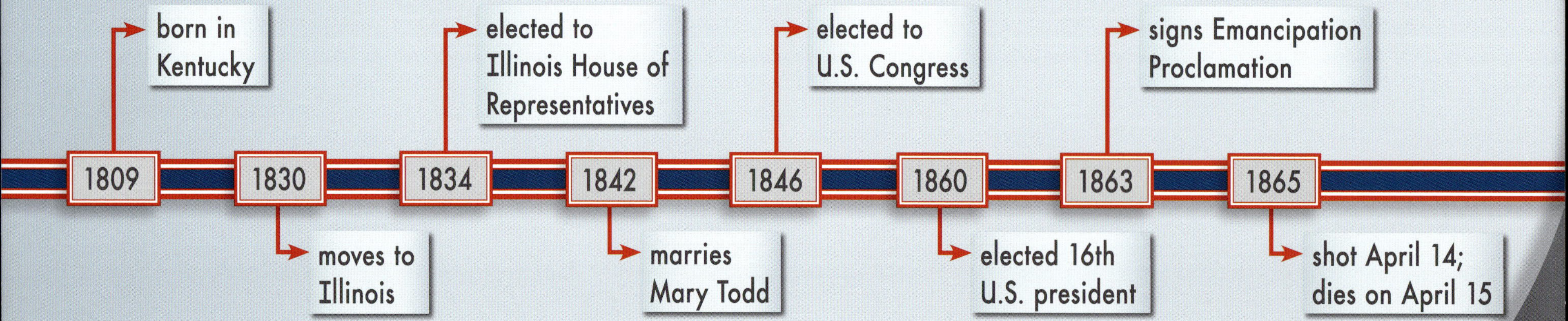

Glossary

Civil War—the battle between states in the North and South that led to the end of slavery in the United States

Congress—the elected government body of the United States that makes laws

debate—to have a discussion between two sides with different ways of thinking on a subject

Emancipation Proclamation—an important paper signed by President Abraham Lincoln during the Civil War, which aimed to free slaves in areas under Confederate control

issue—an idea or need that is talked about by citizens and government leaders

politics—the debate and activity involved in governing a country

slavery—the owning of other people; slaves are forced to work without pay

Read More

Abnett, Dan. *Abraham Lincoln and The Civil War.* Jr. Graphic Biographies. New York: PowerKids Press, 2007.

Gosman, Gillian. *Abraham Lincoln.* Life Stories. New York: PowerKids Press, 2011.

St. George, Judith. *Stand Tall, Abe Lincoln.* A Turning Point Book. New York: Philomel Books, 2008.

Internet Sites

FactHound offers a safe, fun way to find Internet sites related to this book. All of the sites on FactHound have been researched by our staff.

Here's all you do:

Visit *www.facthound.com*

Type in this code: 9781429687355

Index

Word Count: 333
Grade: 1
Early-Intervention Level: 23